There is power in color.
Manipulated emotions, perfect distractions
All-knowing and unforgiving

Devoid of color, we find the truth
Stripped of light, we see in the Raw.

In this pursuit,

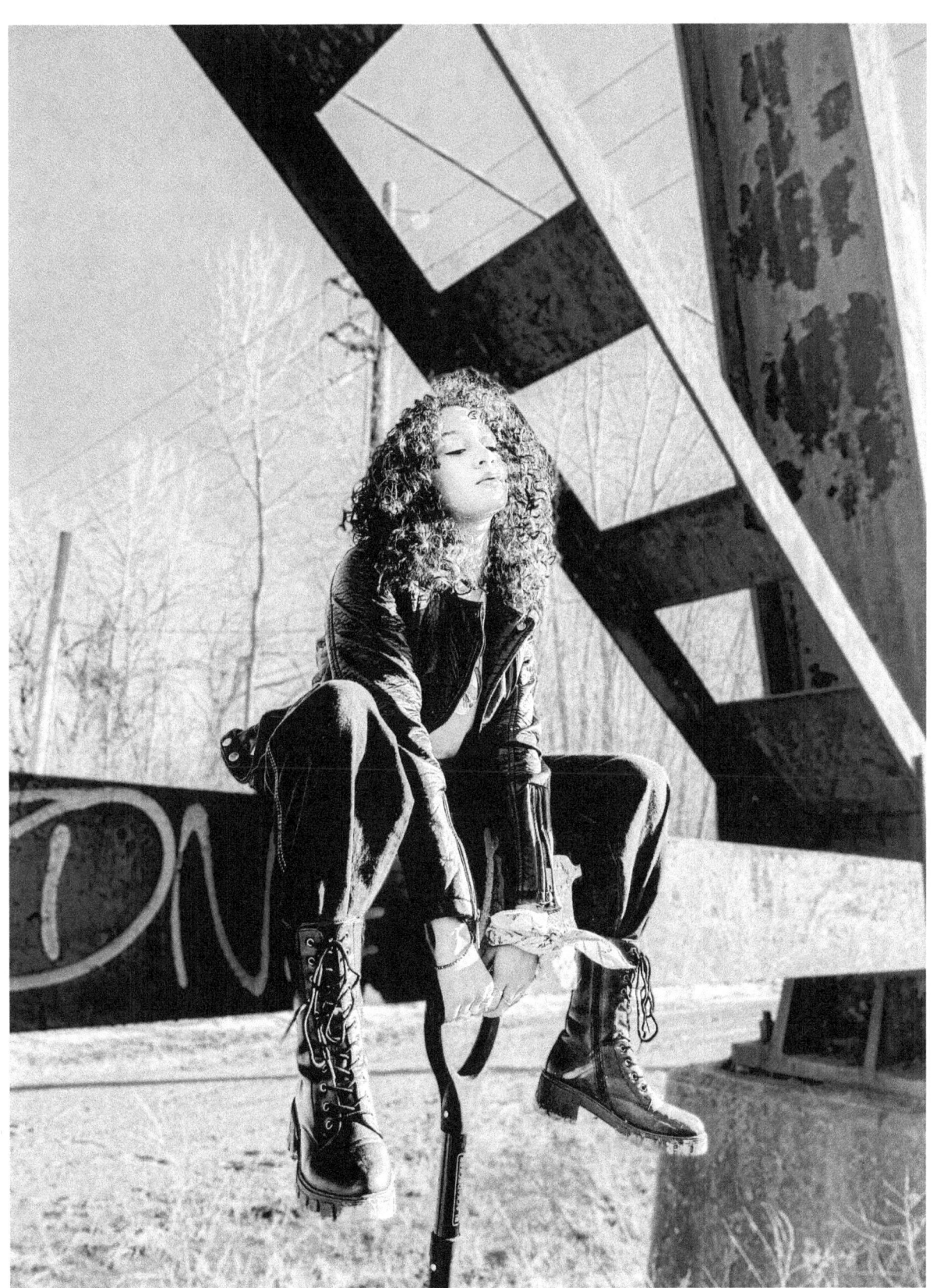

we must first endure.

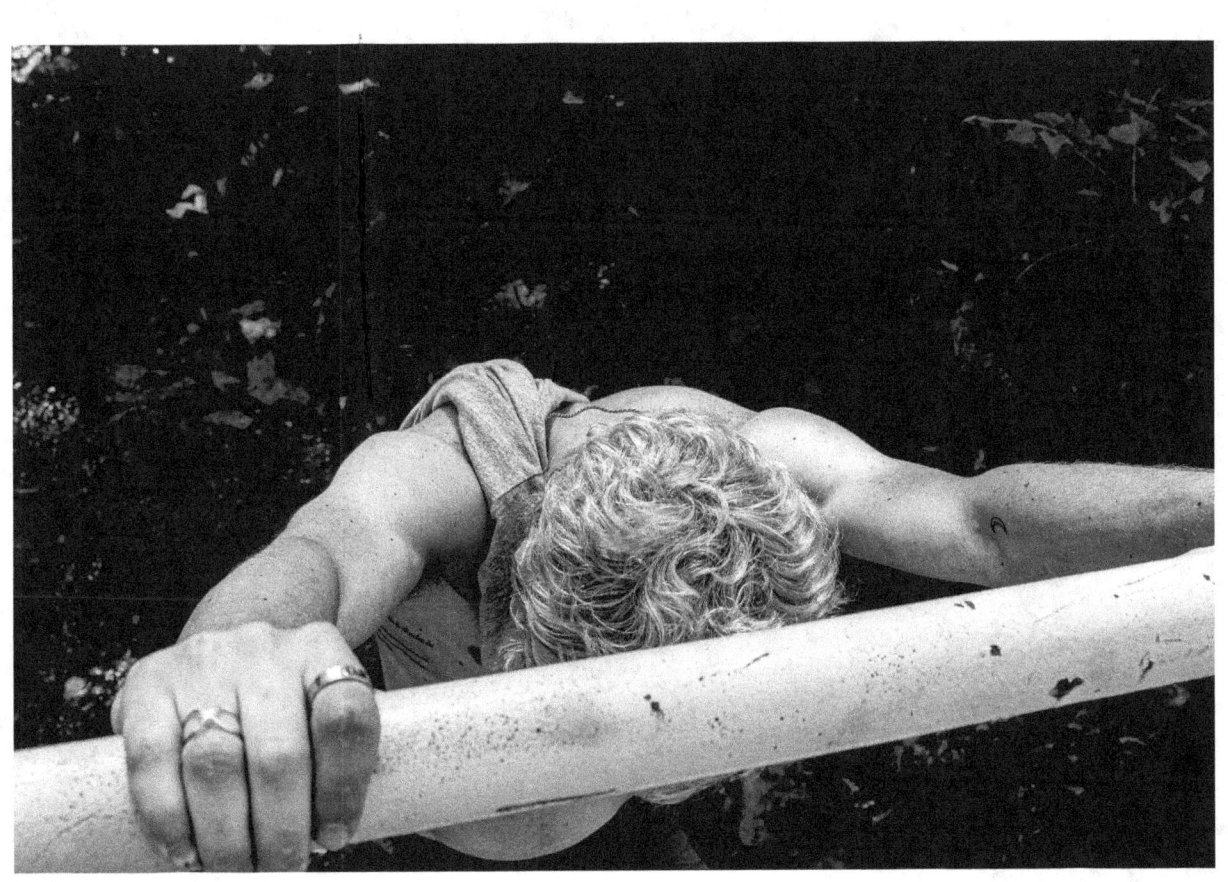

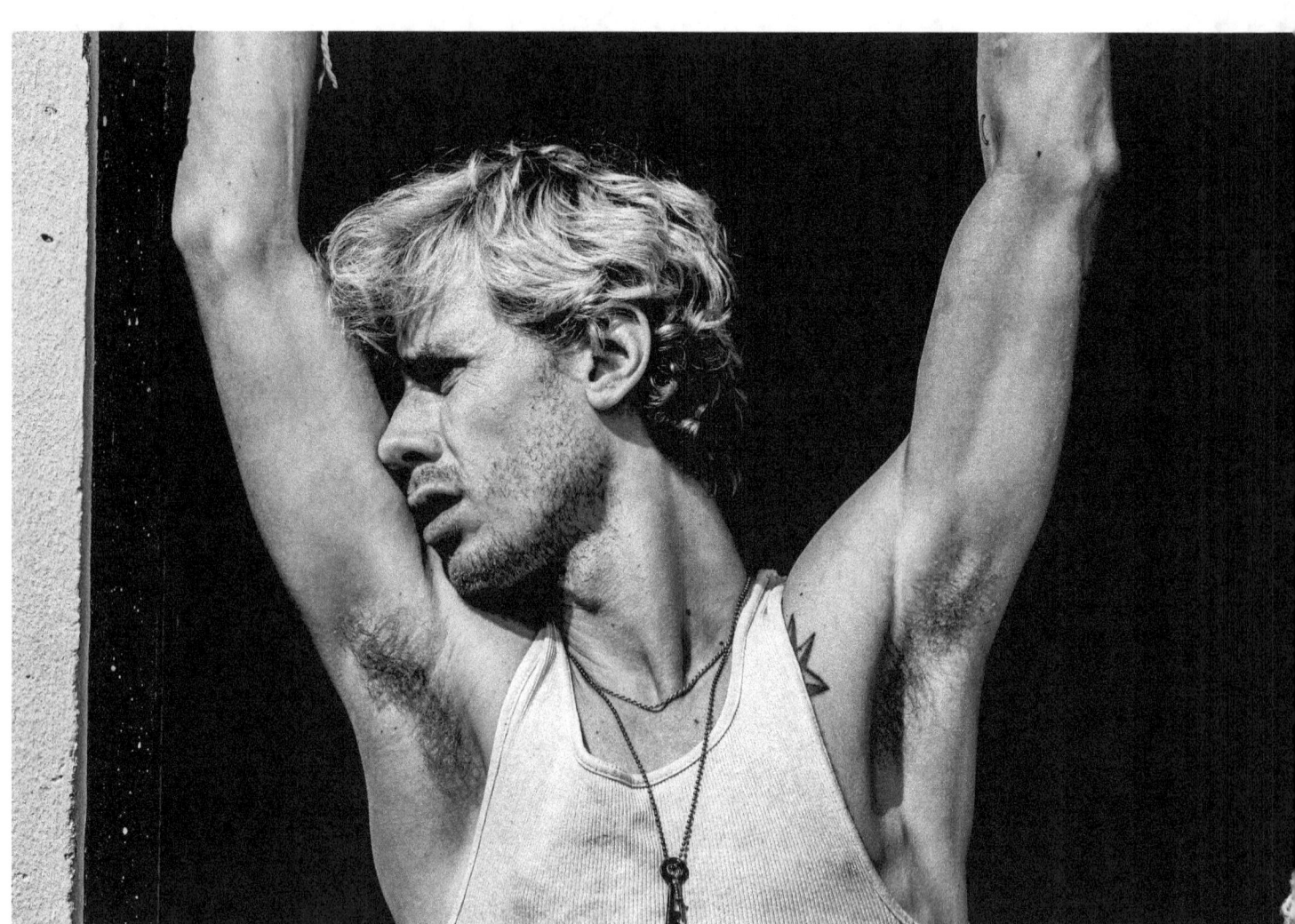

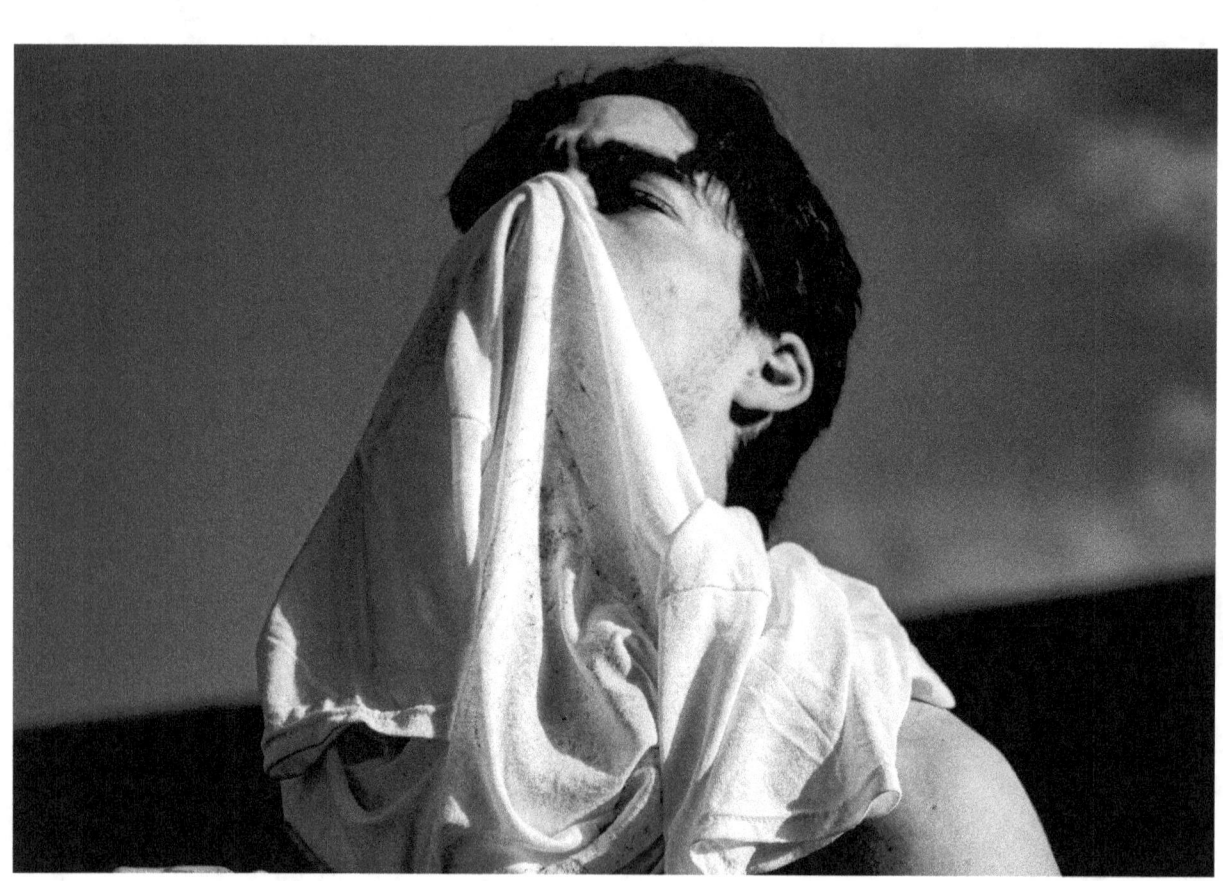

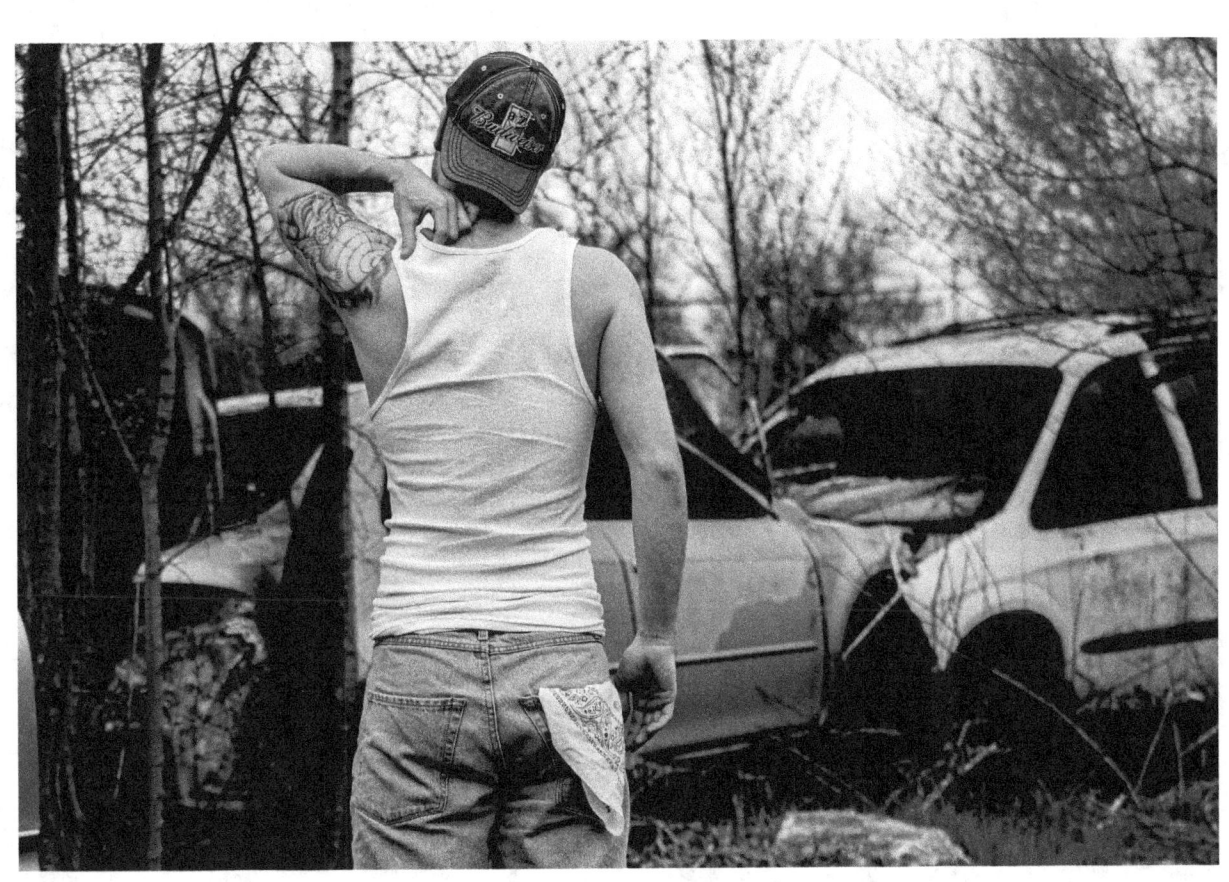

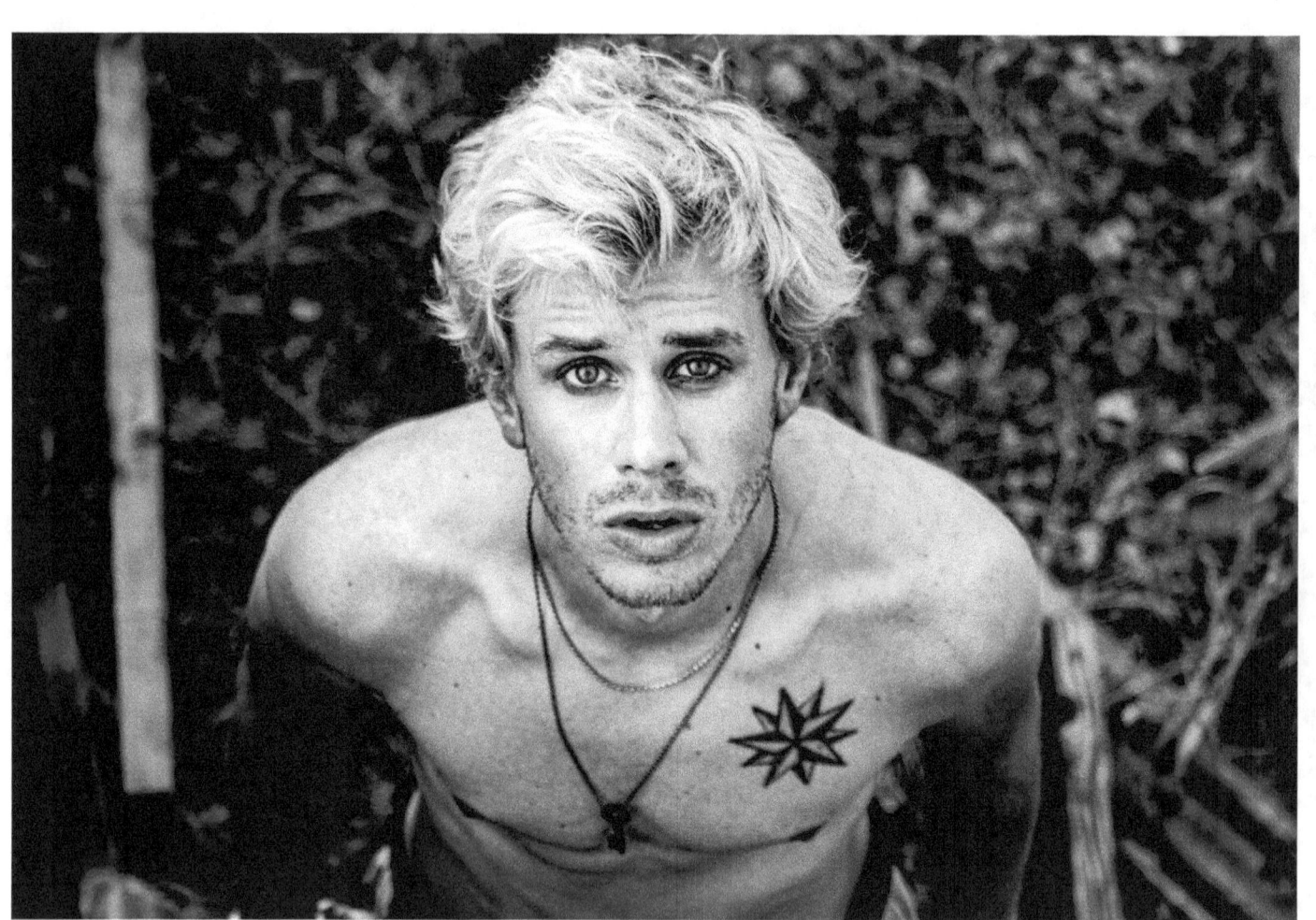

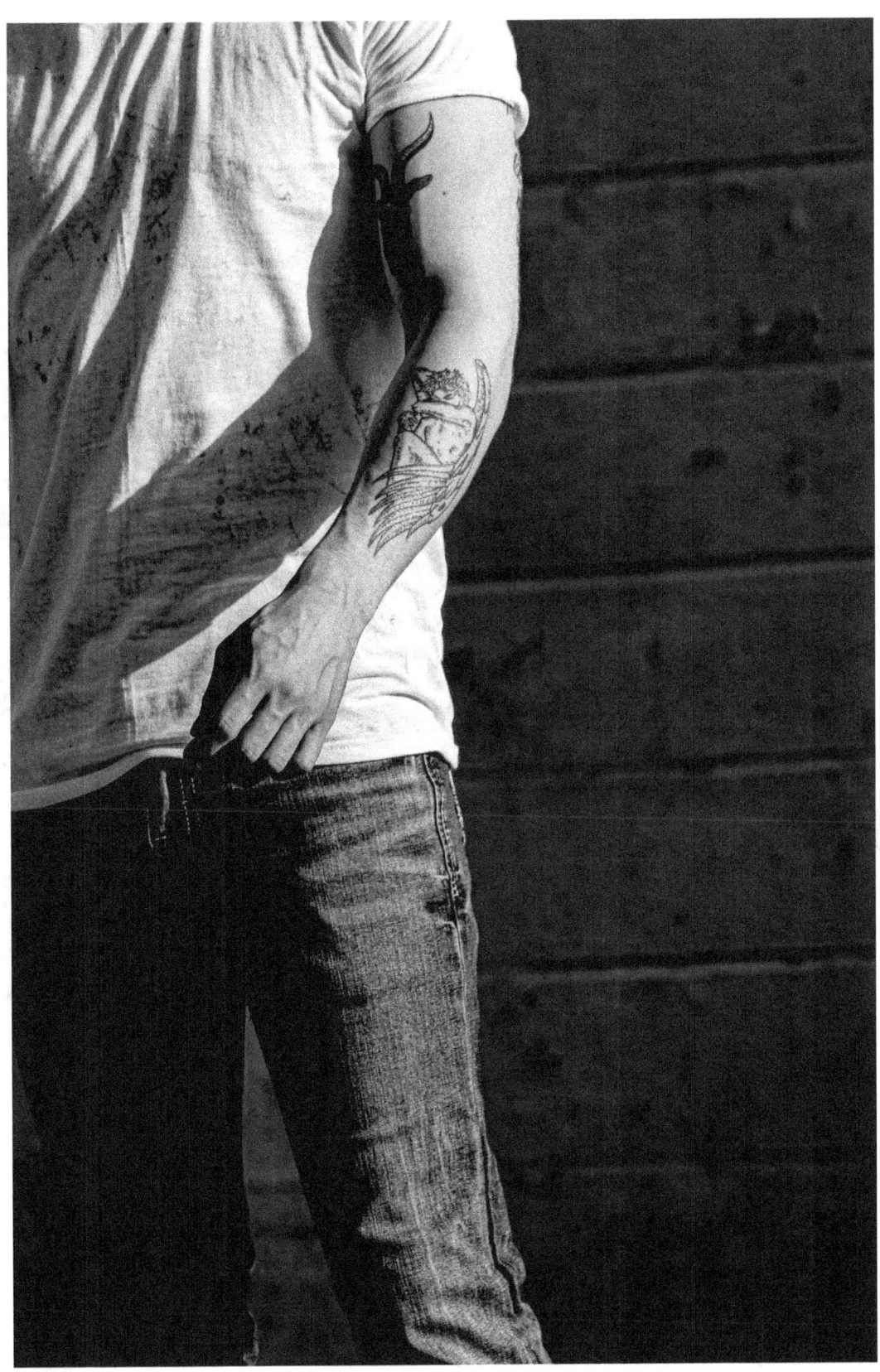

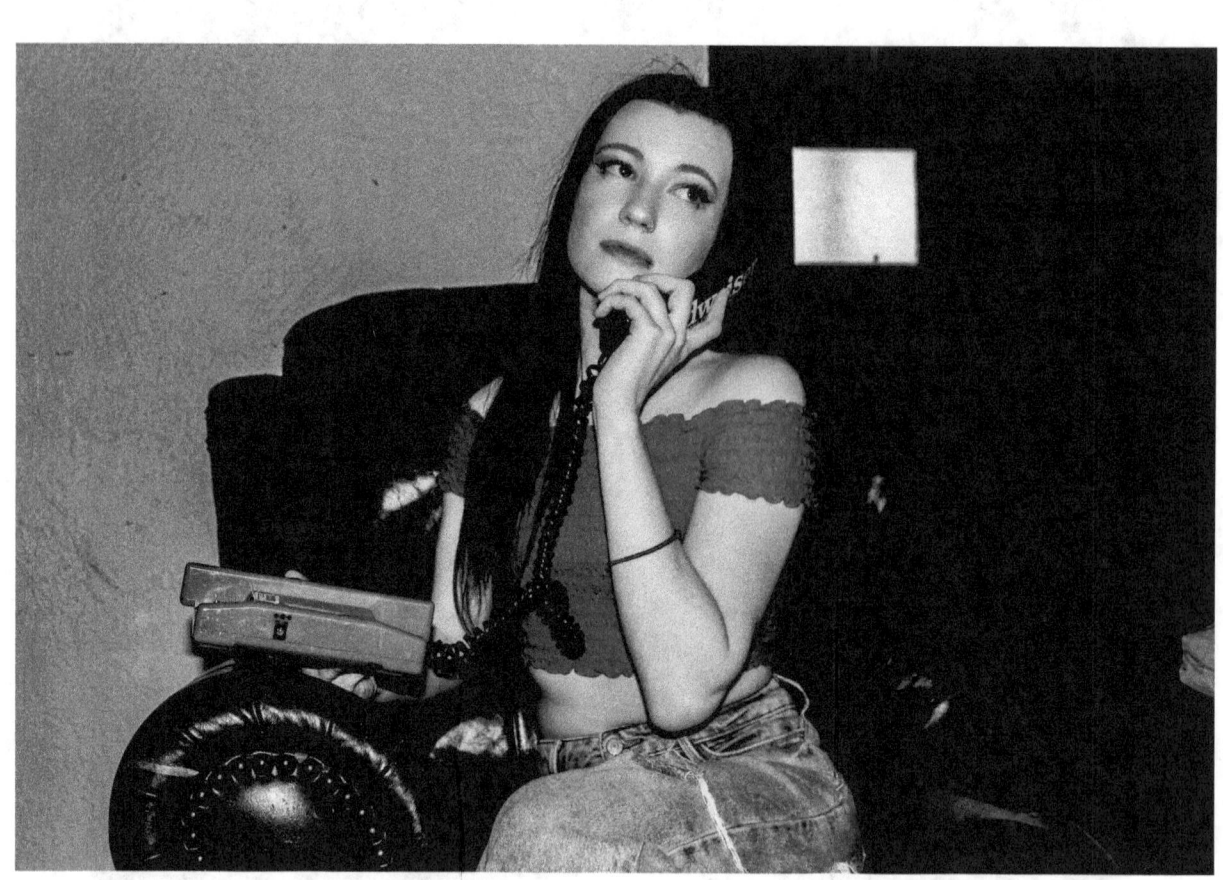

This world

we suffer,

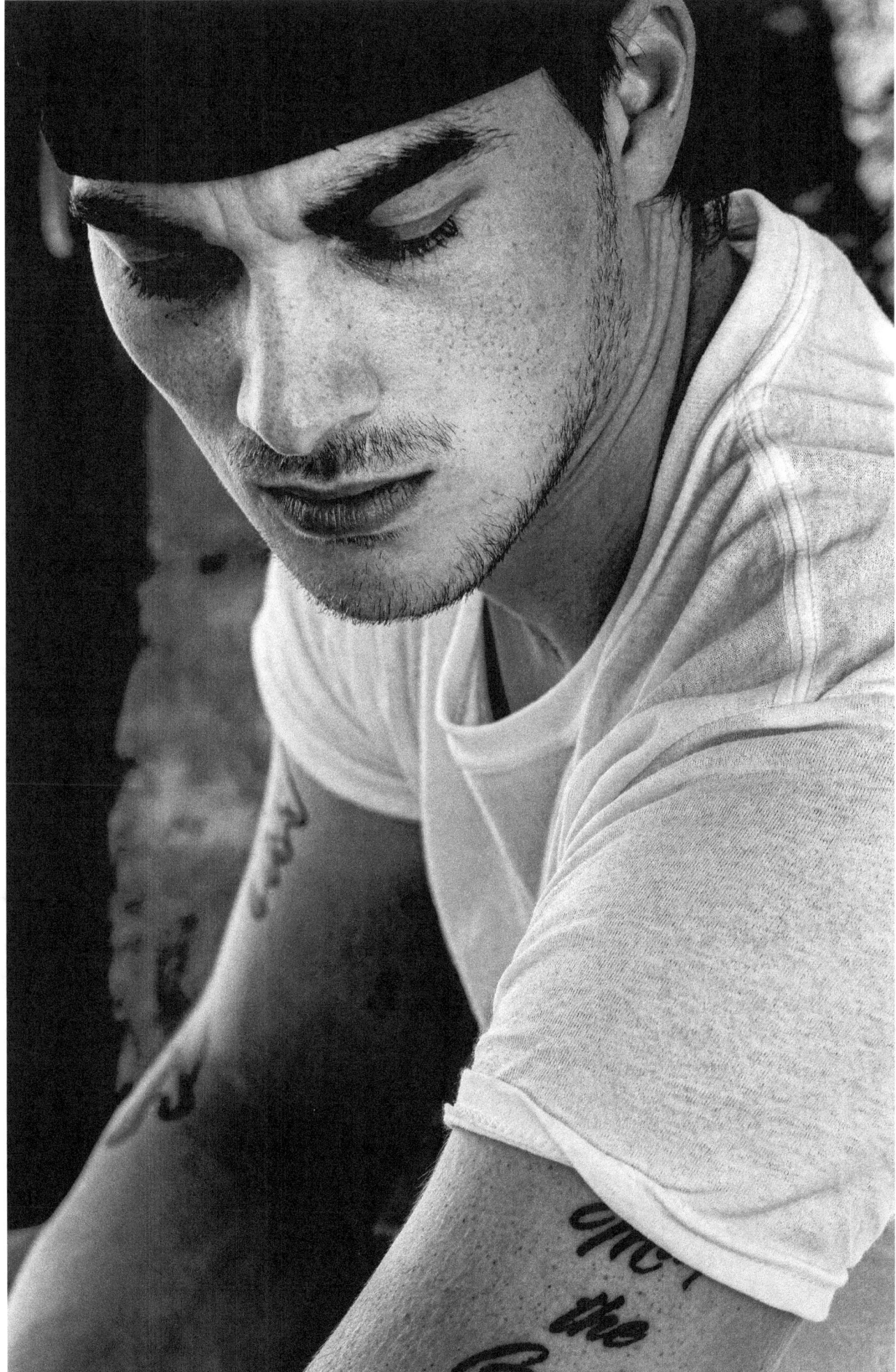

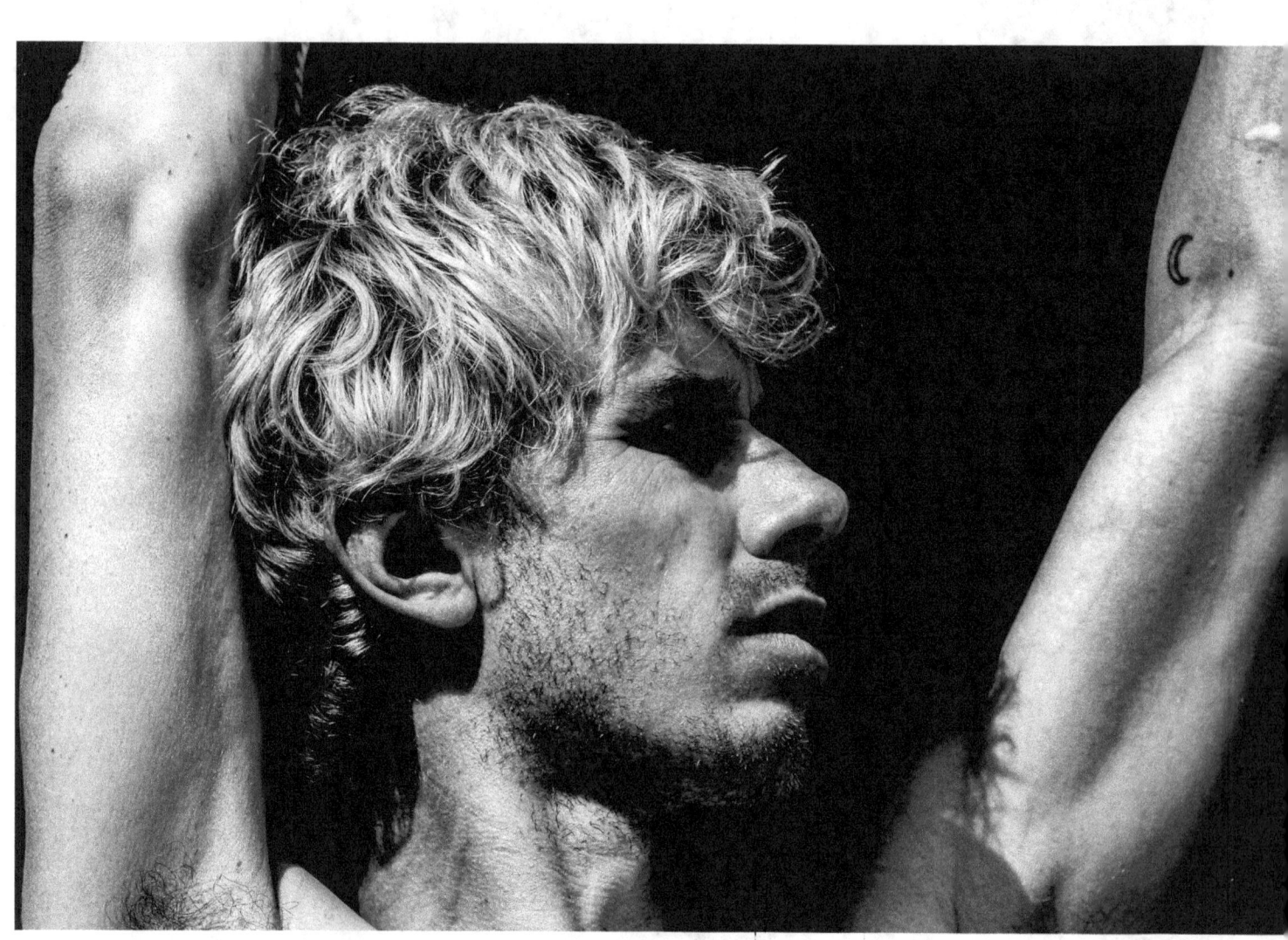

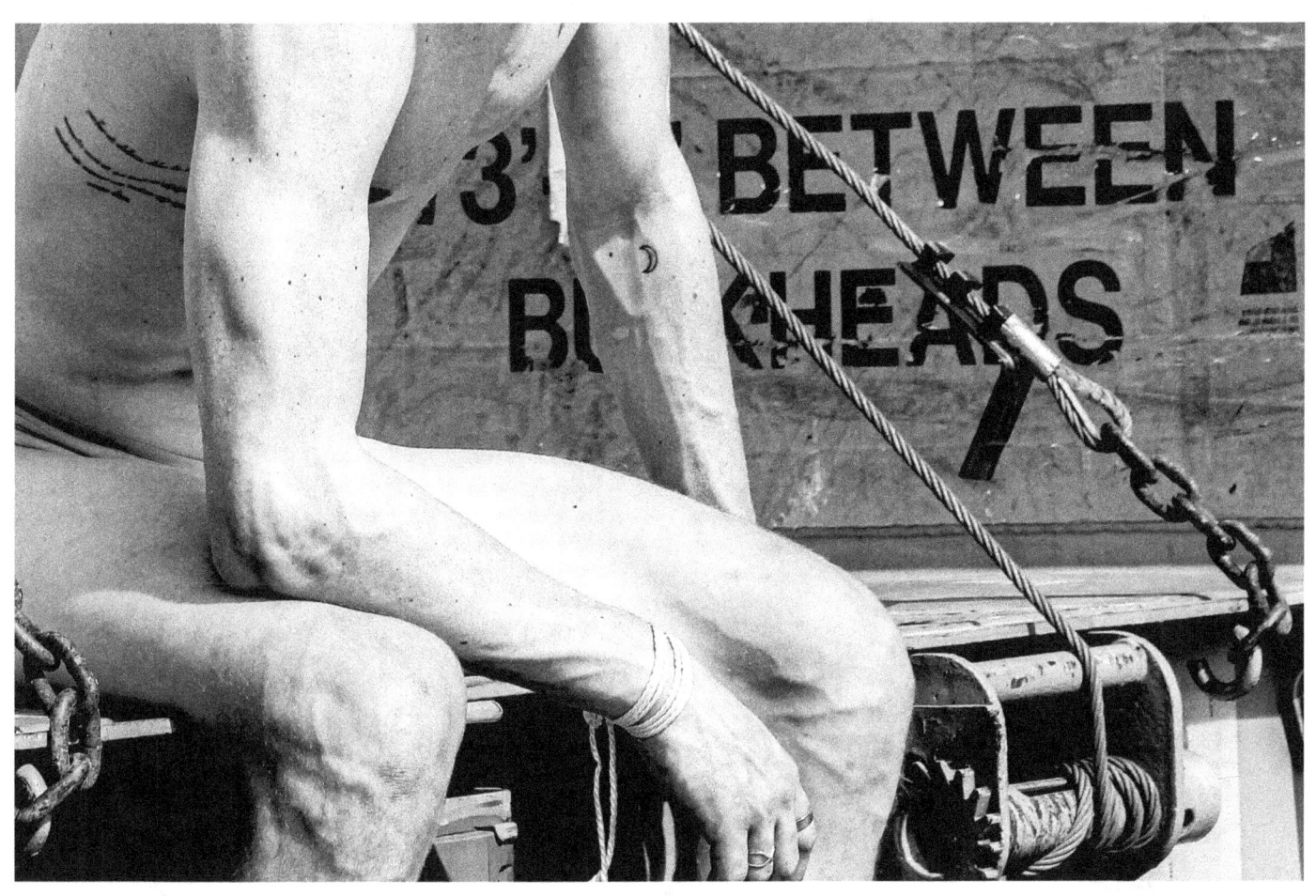

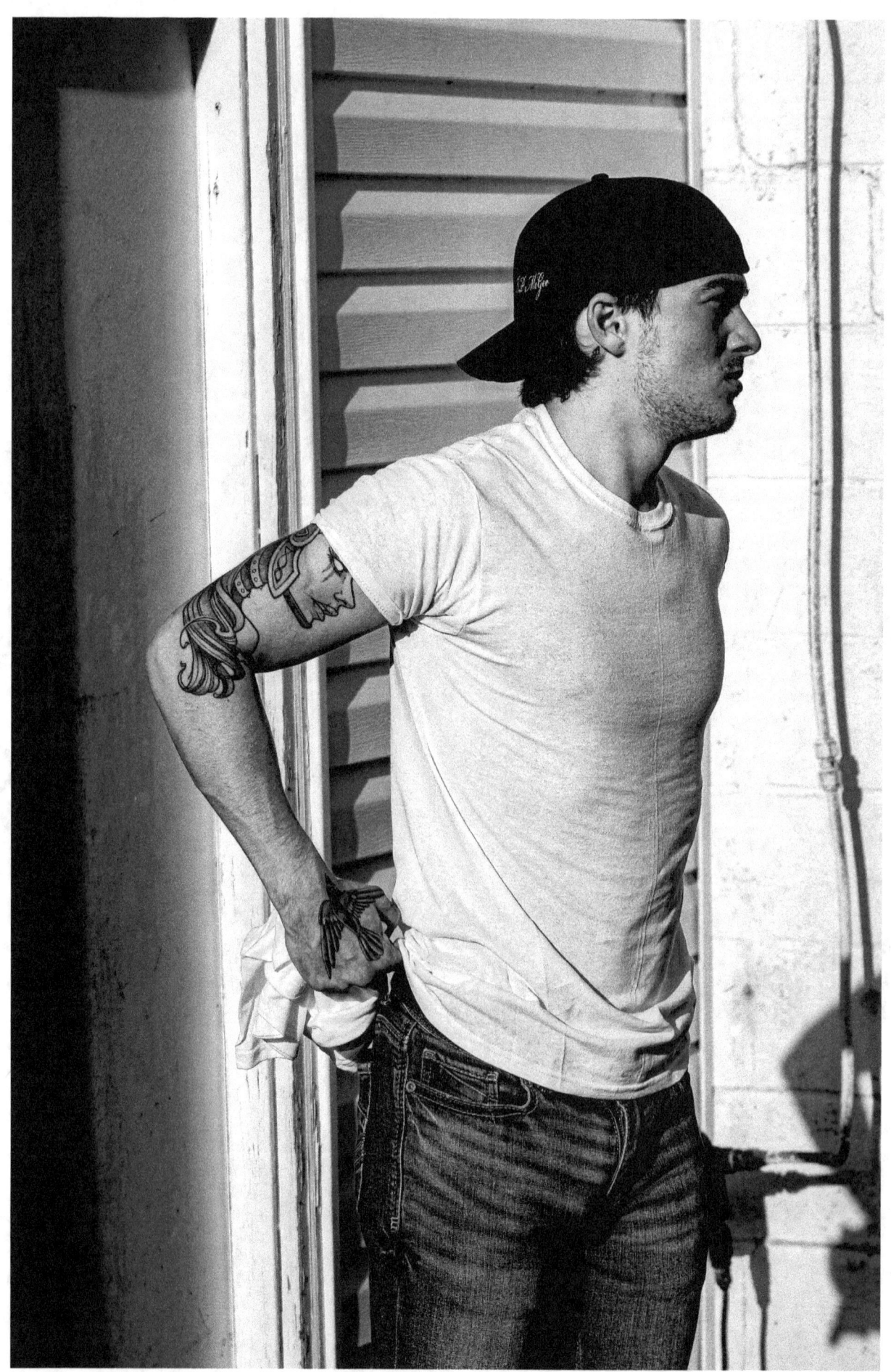

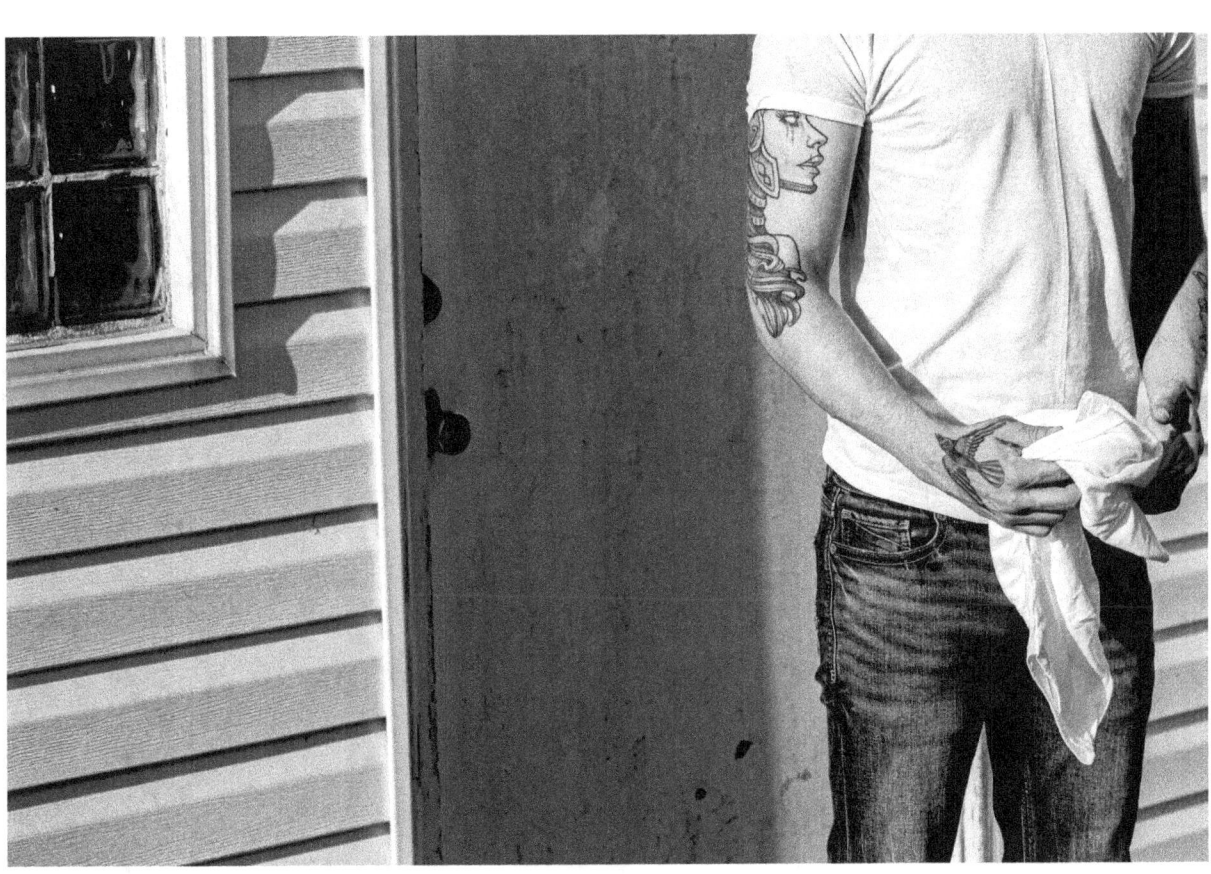

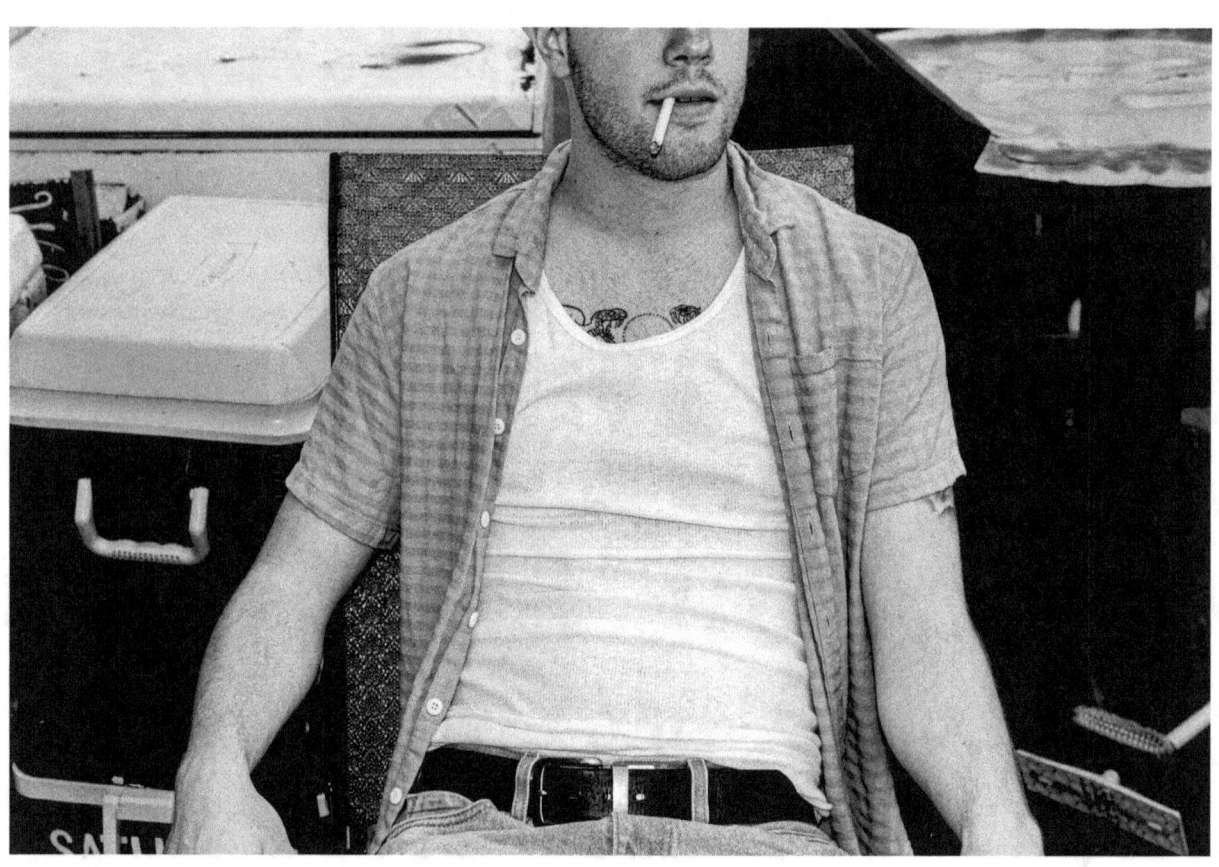

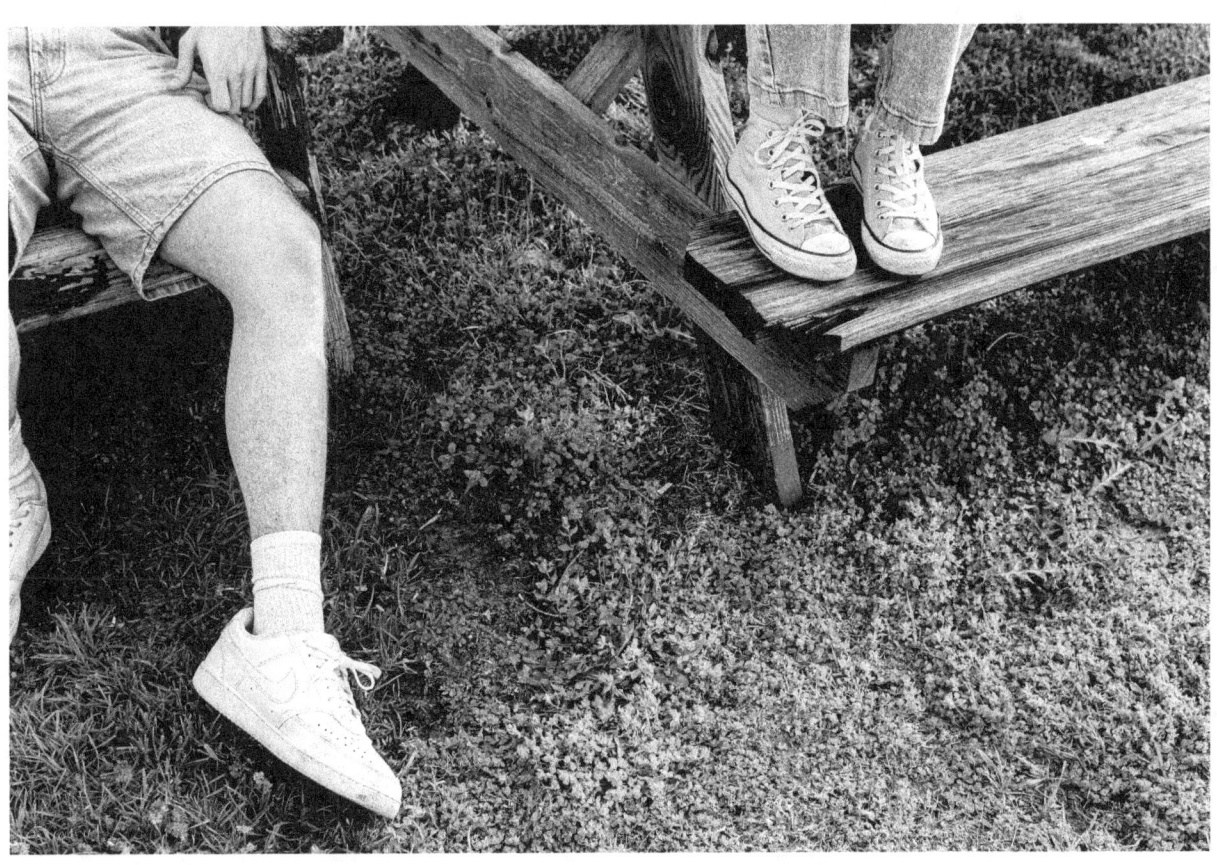

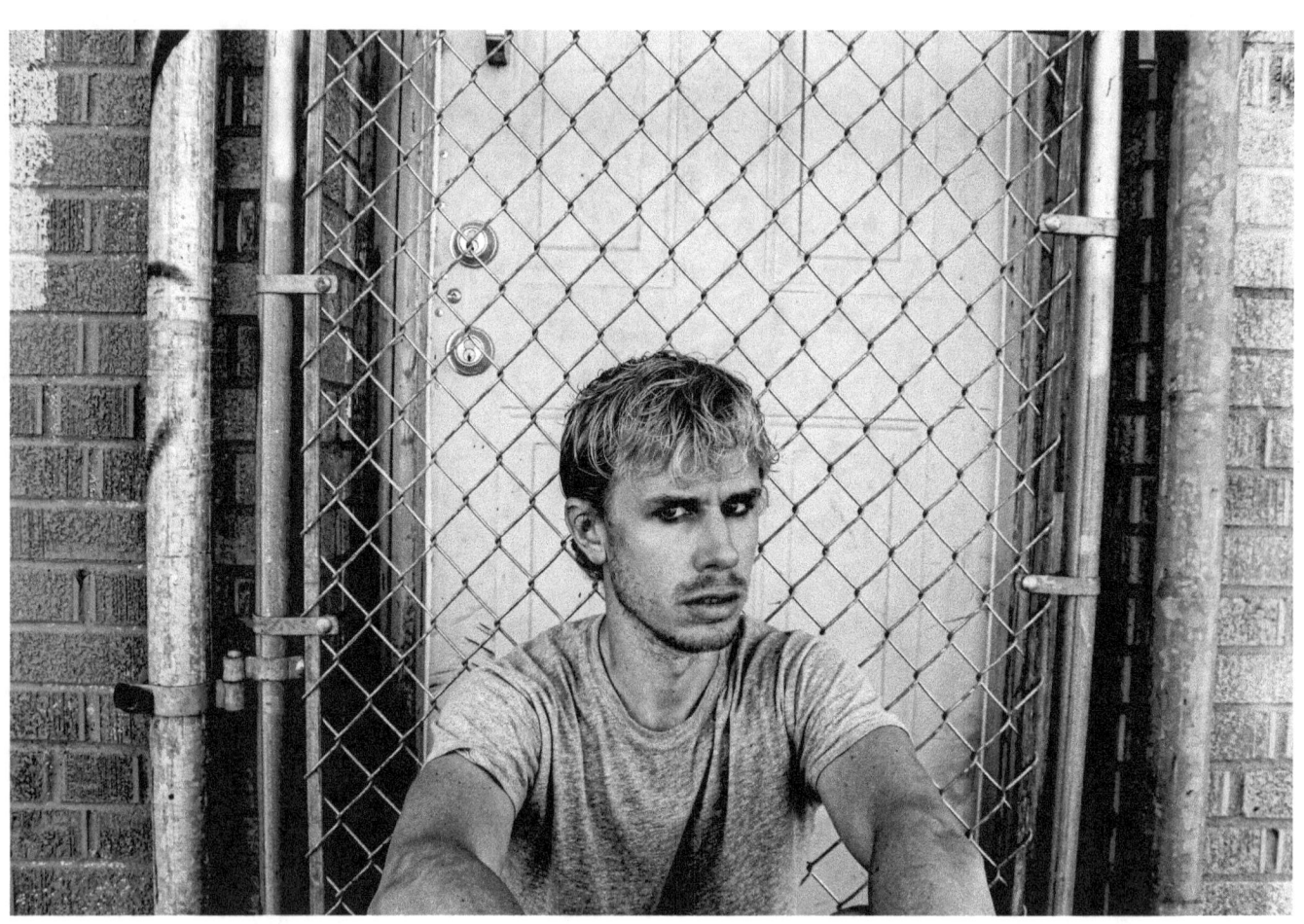

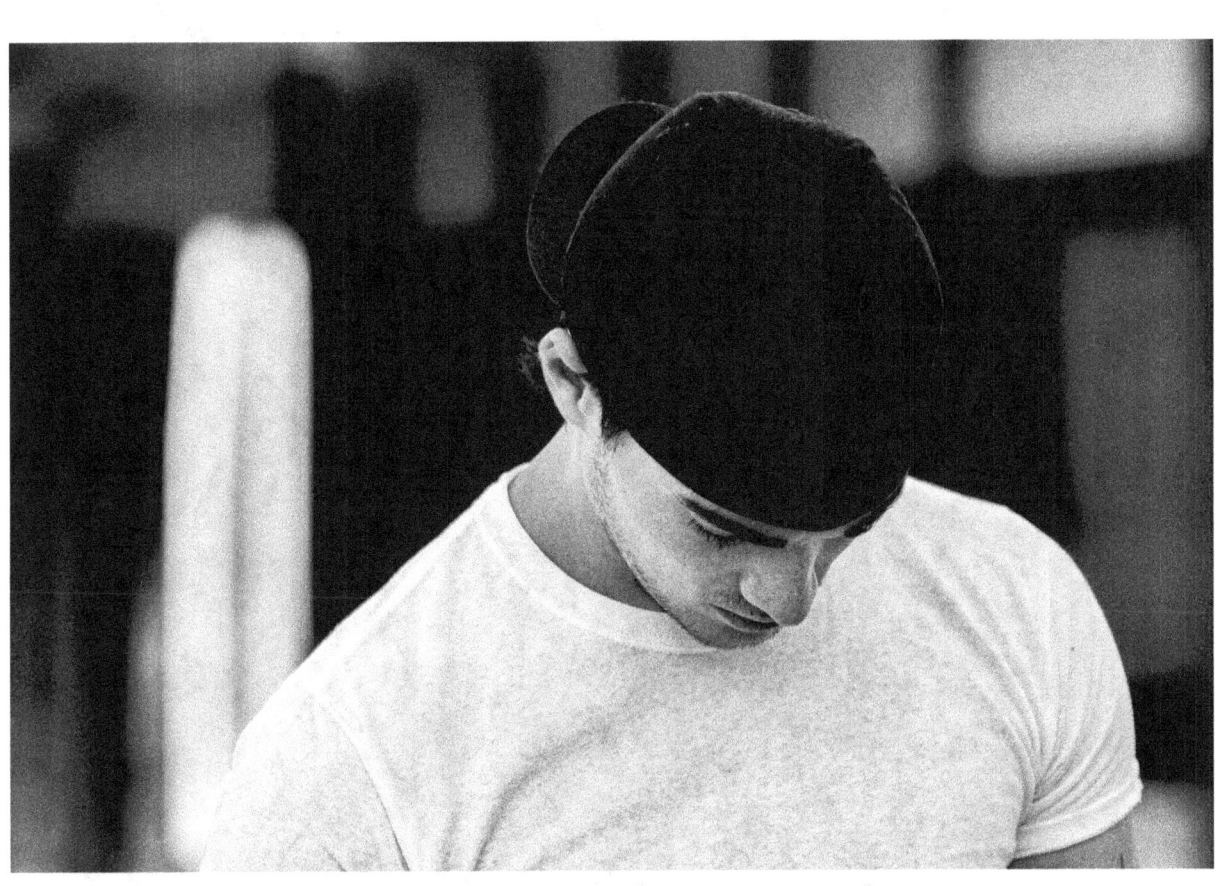

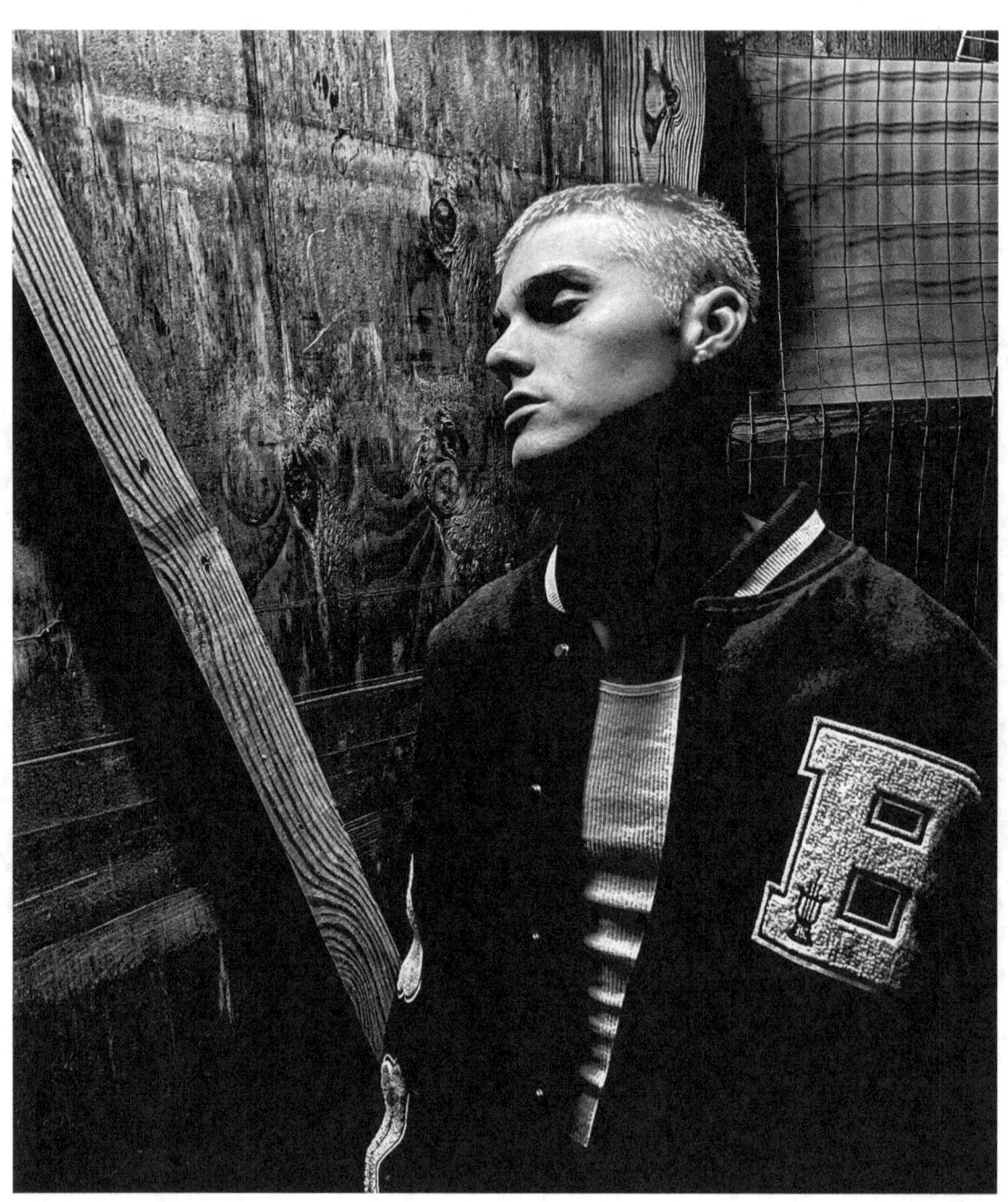

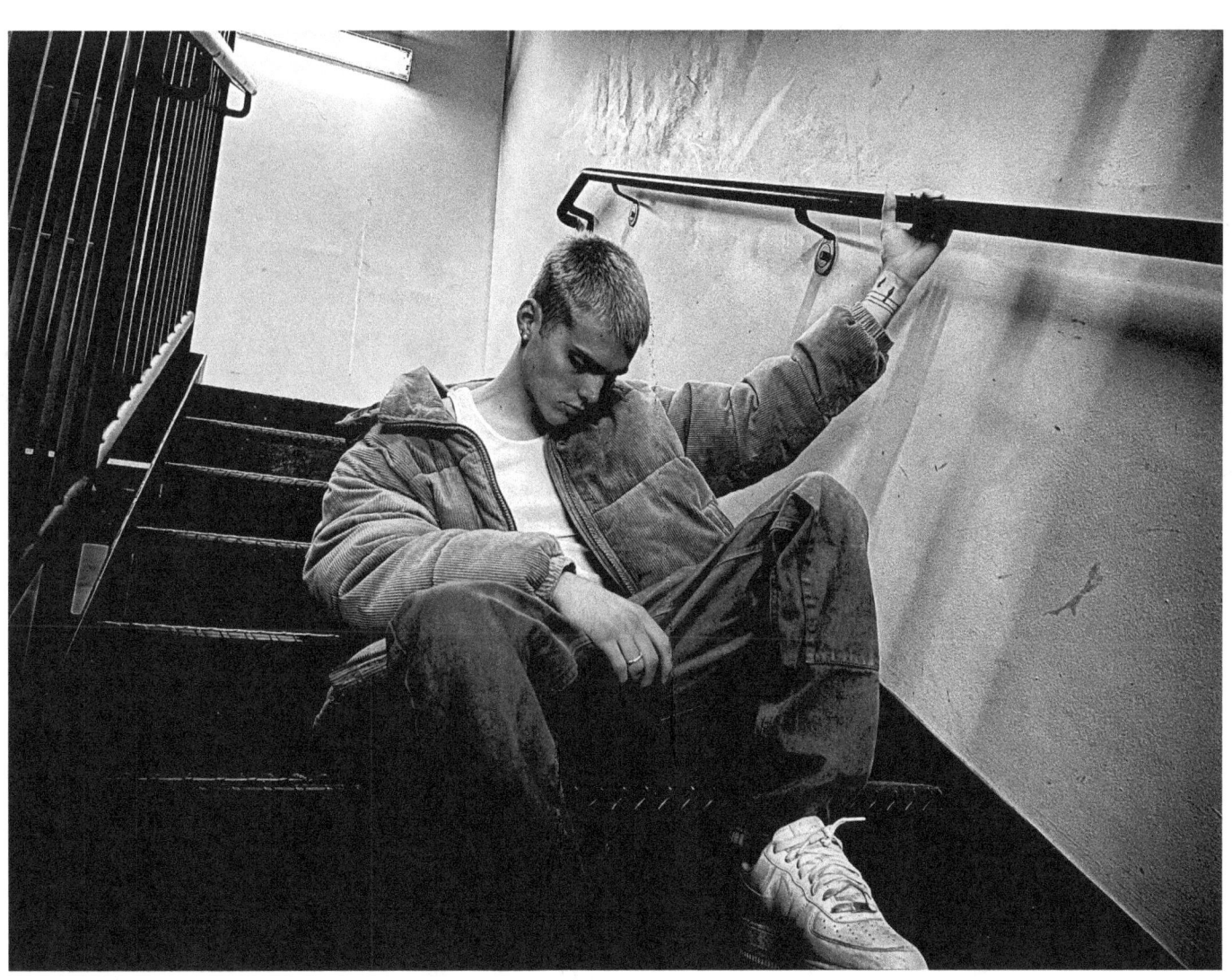

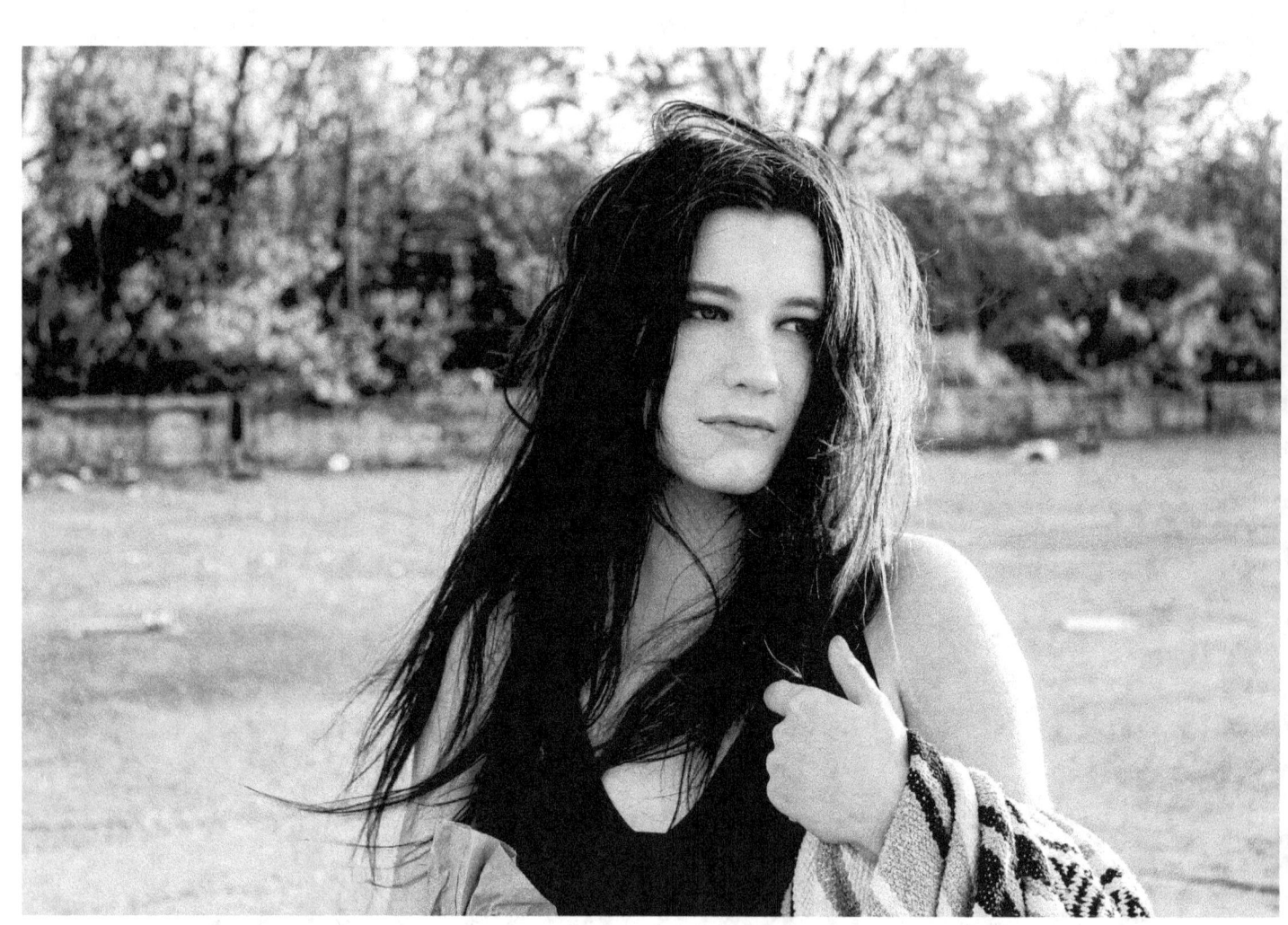

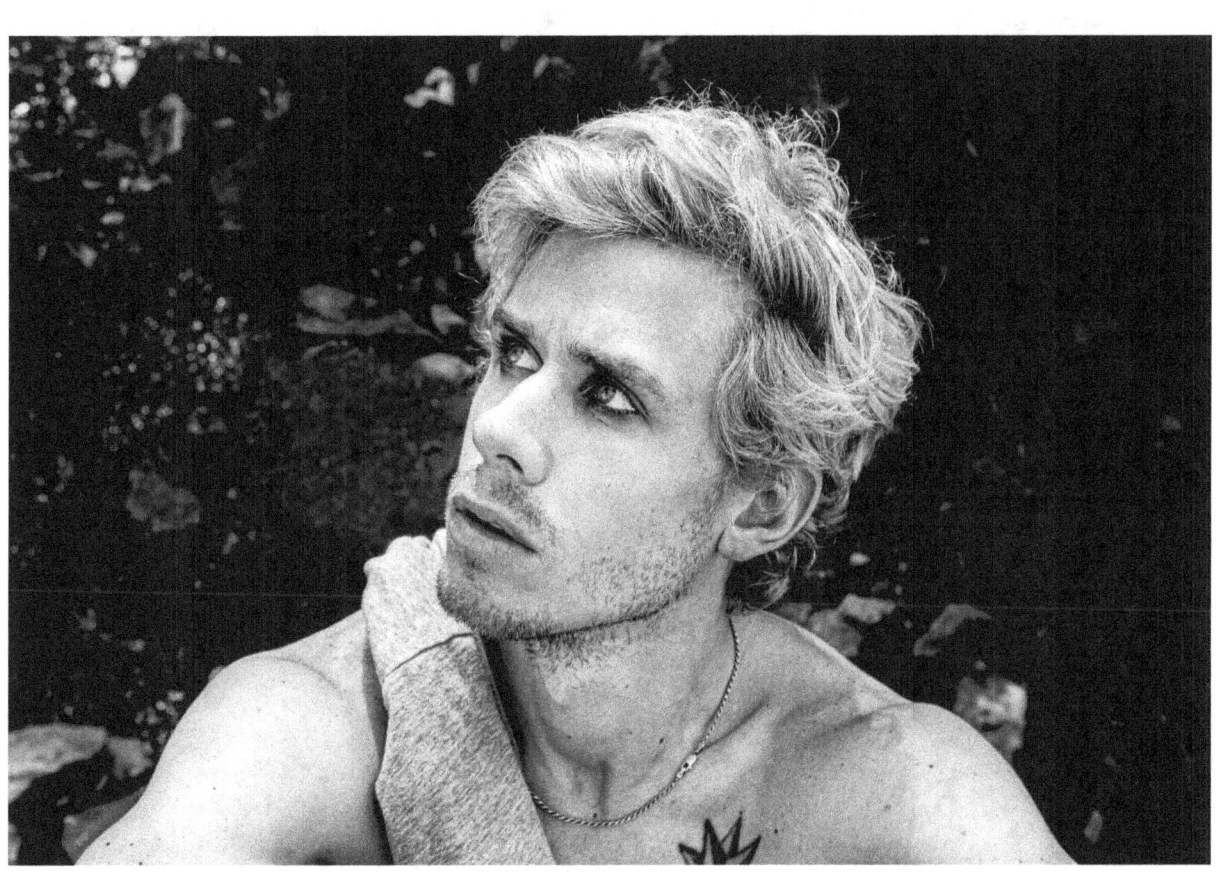

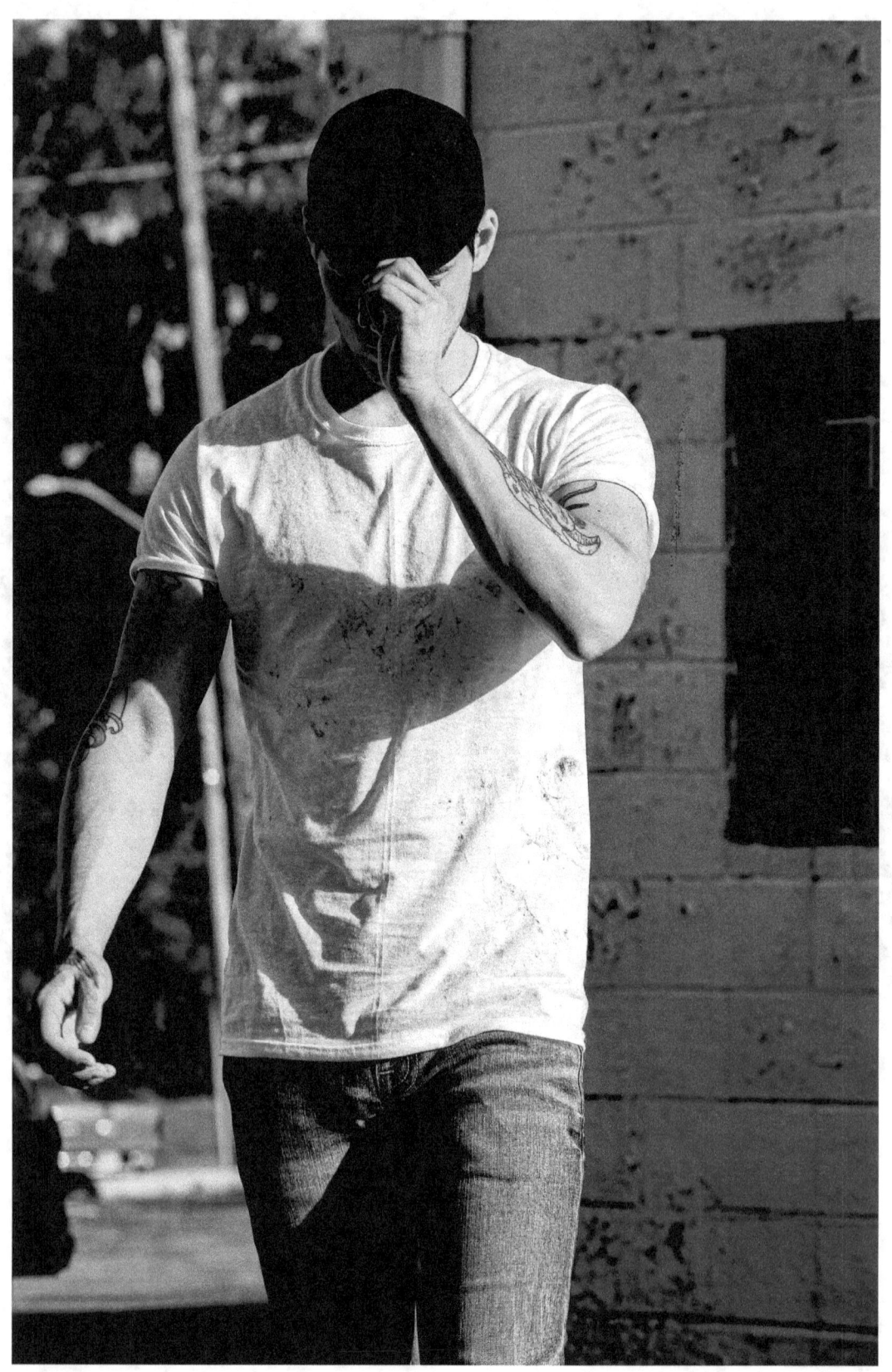

and this heart we must withstand.

Photographs by
Cameron Lee Brown

In Order of Appearance:
DevinJ.
KaitlynB.
JoshuaG.
JosephE.
KateW.
JacobS.